ELITE
DEFENDERS

SPECIAL
FORCES

Sarah Levete

W
FRANKLIN WATTS
LONDON • SYDNEY

Franklin Watts
First published in Great Britain in 2016 by The Watts Publishing Group

Credits
Series Editors: Sarah Eason and Jennifer Sanderson
Series Designers: Paul Myerscough and Simon Borrough

Picture credits: Department of Defense (DoD): 30, 27t, Cpl. Raymond D. Petersen III 20, Petty Officer 2nd Class Shauntae Hinkle-Lymas 25, Pfc. Codey Underwood 38–39, Senior Master Sgt. Dennis W. Goff, Air National Guard 24, Sgt. Pete Thibodeau 35, Spc. Joel LeMaistre 19, Tech. Sgt. John Asselin 29; Dreamstime: Brett Critchley 15, Julius Costache 14t; Shutterstock: Aaron Amat 11, Connei 13, CreativeHQ 9, Katarzyna Mazurowska 8, Militarist 31, VanderWolf Images 5; US Air Force: Airman 1st Class Marc I. Lane 23, Robbin Cresswell 3, 12, Tech. Sgt. Adrian Cadiz 32, Tech. Sgt. Scott Reed 36; US Air National Guard: Master Sgt. Mark C. Olsen 34; US Army: 28, Pfc. David Devich 4, Pfc. Gabriel Segura 17, Pfc. Steven Young 6, 7, Spc. Connor Mendez 22, Staff Sgt. Bryan Henson 27c, Staff Sgt. Jeremy D. Crisp 37; US Marine Corps: Cpl. Lauren Whitney 16; US Navy: Journalist 2nd Class Sarah Bibbs 42, Petty Officer 2nd Class Eli J. Medellin 1, US Navy Photographer's Mate 2nd Class Eric S. Logsdon 21; Wikimedia Commons: Flophila88 43, National Archives and Records Administration 40, Snapperjack 14b, US Navy/Mass Communication Specialist 2nd Class (AW) Johansen Laurel 41, 45.

Dewey number: 356.1'6
ISBN: 978 1 4451 5035 2

Printed in China

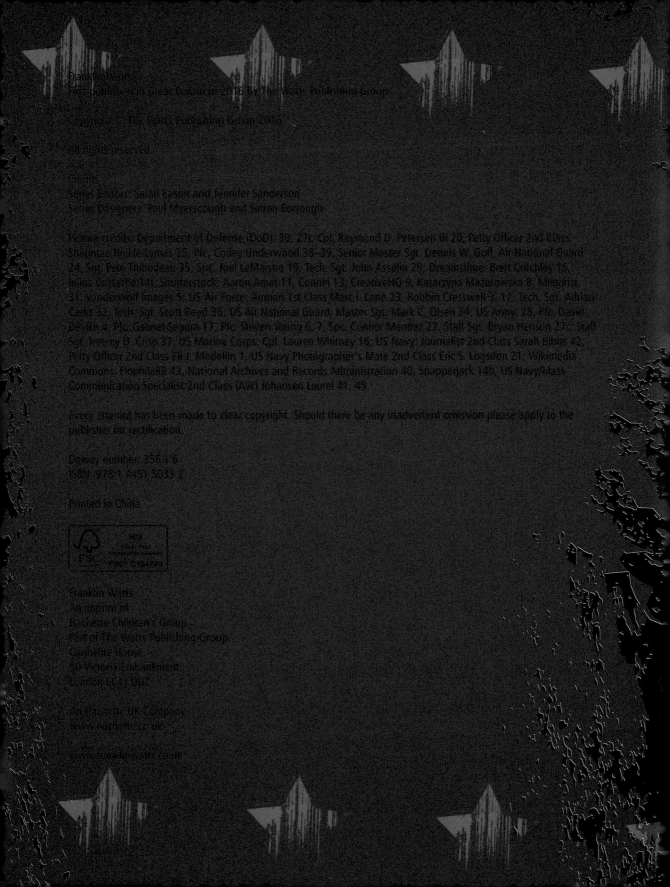

Franklin Watts
An imprint of
Hachette Children's Group
Part of The Watts Publishing Group
Carmelite House
50 Victoria Embankment
London EC4Y 0DZ

An Hachette UK Company
www.hachette.co.uk

www.franklinwatts.co.uk

Contents

CHAPTER 1:
Special Forces

Special Forces teams are trained to deal with unpredictable situations.

Imagine being dropped from a helicopter in the dead of night above hostile enemy territory. Imagine being responsible for the safety of your team. If any one of you makes a mistake, your whole team might be captured by a deadly and ruthless enemy. This is real life for members of the world's Special Forces.

Who is brave and skilled enough to risk life and limb for the sake of their country? Who can train for months under the harshest conditions and still perform at their best? The answer is the men and women who are members of the Special Forces, the world's elite military groups.

Read on to find out what it takes to be a member of the Special Forces. This book is about some of the most courageous and skilled men and women in the military who make up the Special Forces. These forces are sent on top-secret and dangerous missions around the world, defending their country and working for the safety of others.

Special Forces

The term 'Special Forces' refers to a variety of specialised forces working in all areas of the armed services. Each force is made up of highly trained individuals, who have to demonstrate outstanding skill and ability to work in the elite team.

Facing danger

THINK LIKE A SPECIAL FORCES OPERATIVE

The Green Berets are the men and women who make up the USA's special army ground force. Wearing trademark green berets, members of this elite Special Forces team are prepared to scale rugged mountains, trek through deep forests and drop from hovering helicopters to successfully complete their missions.

Also known as the US Army Special Forces, the Green Berets are sent on some of the US force's most dangerous missions. They are sent into hostile territory to gather crucial intelligence, known as intel, and then make their escape, unobserved.

As well as working in combat situations and gathering important information, the Green Berets train the military of other 'friendly' nations. Sharing their expert skills enables other less experienced soldiers to then defend and protect their own countrymen and women.

ACT LIKE A GREEN BERET

Hearts and minds

Only the fittest and bravest can join the Green Berets. However, the Green Berets division is not just about physical strength. Each member must speak another language and is trained in communication skills. These are essential for the Green Berets' important work in gathering intel and offering practical help when needed. For example, in the 1990s, the Green Berets helped refugees fleeing the war in Rwanda, Central Africa, to reach safety in refugee camps. They used their skills to help set up the camps.

In training

A United States Navy SEAL (which stands for Sea, Air and Land) works as a part of a small team, carrying out missions in some of the world's most hostile environments. A SEAL never works alone, and a SEAL is never left alone. SEALs are unbeatable when it comes to working in thrashing seas, boggy marshes or fast-flowing rivers. Although SEALs specialise in missions on, under or near water, they also work in other challenging environments.

SEAL training pushes members to the limits to make sure that the few who make it through the 30 months of physical and mental challenges will be able to survive on real missions. SEAL recruits have to prove they can cope with the demands and risks of this elite team. They must be able to swim 100 metres with their hands and feet bound. They have to run across a beach, carrying a 4.6-metre rigid inflatable boat, called a Zodiac, over their heads while wearing heavy kit.

Dark missions

SEALs are often used in hostage rescue, capture of targets and special research. Many missions take place in the dead of night, to ensure enemies are caught by surprise. The darkness hides the SEALs from view, but they need to see where they are going. Night vision goggles help them to find their way and locate enemy targets in the pitch black.

Night vision goggles

THINK LIKE A SEAL

TAKE THE TEST!

Could you be in the Special Forces?

How much have you learnt about the Green Berets or SEALs? Use the information you have read so far to answer the following questions:

Q1. What is the United States' special army ground force also known as?

Q2. What skill must you have before you apply to be a Green Beret?

Q3. What equipment do SEALs use to help them to see on night missions?

Q4. Which team of Navy SEALs is often used to rescue hostages?

Q5. How many metres must a SEAL be able to swim with bound hands and legs?

Q6. Why do Green Berets need to speak more than one language?

Q7. What is a Zodiac?

Q8. How long is the basic SEAL training?

ANSWERS

CHAPTER 2:
Secret Armies

The Special Forces need to be kept as secret as possible. The operations are often carried out with the fewest people knowing the details of the mission. This protects the operatives and increases the chance of success by taking their enemy by surprise.

Special Forces are dispatched to deal with some of the most dangerous missions, such as hostage recovery and strikes on enemy targets. Each member of these elite teams excels in a particular skill. This ensures that every team is made up of people with the expert knowledge needed to survive the toughest challenges.

Secret
mission

Small units of Special Forces are sent to find information and to observe the enemy and territory before an attack. This is called reconnaissance, or recon. It can involve hiding out in enemy land and staying hidden for days. That means no talking, cooking or any other action that could alert the enemy.

Highly skilled

Many Special Forces operatives are skilled in different languages, so they can work and live among local people to gain their trust. For example, during the war in Afghanistan, knowing the local language helped to obtain crucial information about the enemy – the Taliban. It also helped to persuade locals to fight with the British and US troops against the enemy.

The modern world faces threats from terrorist groups worldwide. The terrorists often work in groups called cells. The skill and focus of Special Forces ops are essential to prevent terrorist attacks. This work is called counter-terrorism.

THINK LIKE A SPECIAL FORCES OPERATIVE

The SAS

In the United Kingdom, little was known about the British Special Air Service (SAS) until a dramatic siege and rescue operation stunned television viewers.

In 1980, the Iranian Embassy in London was taken over by a ruthless gang. Chaos erupted. There were many people in the embassy at the time; they were taken hostage. Dressed in black, carrying H&K MP5 submachine guns, SAS soldiers leapt across the embassy's balconies and flung themselves through the windows into the embassy. In a flurry of gun fire, they managed to rescue the hostages, apart from one whom a terrorist had killed. Five of the six terrorists were killed and one was captured during the mission, codenamed Operation Nimrod.

The SAS stormed the embassy using stun grenades, explosive devices and guns. The six-day siege ended in 11 minutes.

The Iranian Embassy, London

Top team

The smallest SAS team is made up of four men. This is because in an emergency, two soldiers might be needed to carry out a wounded comrade, with the third providing cover and safety from the enemy.

As well as basic military skills, each SAS soldier specialises in at least one other area. The success of each SAS team depends upon the team having these skills:

★ Languages – these are essential for communicating with foreign troops or local people.

★ Demolitions – being able to use explosives safely and effectively.

★ Medical skills – injuries may occur and if they do, the wounded must be cared for.

★ Communications – soldiers need to communicate with their HQ (headquarters) and other teams, using satellite, radios and code.

THINK LIKE AN SAS SOLDIER

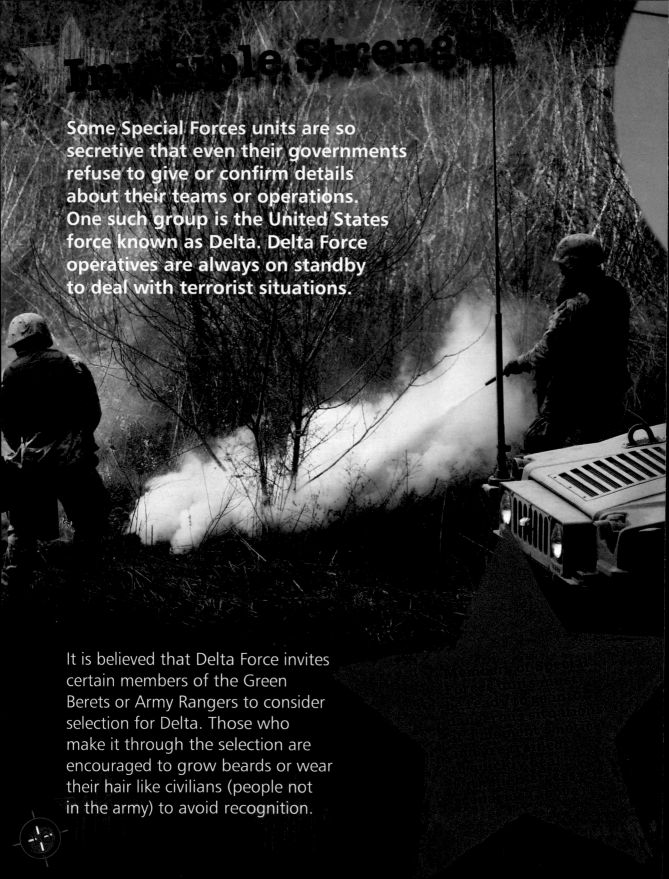

Invisible Strength

Some Special Forces units are so secretive that even their governments refuse to give or confirm details about their teams or operations. One such group is the United States force known as Delta. Delta Force operatives are always on standby to deal with terrorist situations.

It is believed that Delta Force invites certain members of the Green Berets or Army Rangers to consider selection for Delta. Those who make it through the selection are encouraged to grow beards or wear their hair like civilians (people not in the army) to avoid recognition.

Dark fliers

If US Special Forces operatives need to go somewhere fast without detection, Night Stalkers provide the lift. The Night Stalkers is the elite US Army special operations unit that flies helicopters in support of special ops and regular army forces.

Also known as 160th Special Operations Aviation Regiment (SOAR), Night Stalkers fly blacked-out helicopters, avoiding detection by the enemy, and insert men into hostile territory. The helicopters hover close to the ground, so the Special Forces operatives can drop from the craft. Incredibly, the Night Stalkers promise to reach their destination within 30 seconds of their target time.

Inserting the team

THINK LIKE A NIGHT STALKER

TAKE THE TEST!

Are you smart enough to be on the team?

Paying attention is key to being a successful Special Forces operative. You have read about some of the best elite forces, so let's check to see if you have been paying attention to the details. Use the information you have read so far to answer the following questions:

Q1. Why do SAS teams need a minimum of four men?

Q2. Why are Night Stalkers' aircraft specially adapted?

Q3. What is the Night Stalkers' motto?

Q4. Who does Delta invite for selection?

Q5. What submachine guns do the SAS use?

Q6. What colour is the SAS uniform?

Q7. Why are members of Delta Force encouraged to grow beards?

Q8. What do the Night Stalkers promise?

Q9. When did the SAS come to public attention and what was the codename of the operation?

Q10. What is the 160th Special Operations Aviation Regiment more commonly known as?

ANSWERS

CHAPTER 3:
Training the Best

Each Special Forces unit has its own training regime, but no one should apply for any of them unless they are already in the military. There is no room for weakness in the Special Forces. One operative's weakness can cause the failure of a mission.

Trainees are exposed to the harshest conditions in the world, from the freezing Arctic to roasting deserts. Training to join the Special Forces takes months of gruelling mental and physical endurance – and most recruits will not make it through to qualification. Out of an average intake of 125 candidates who apply for the SAS, only ten will make it past the extreme selection process.

Every Special Forces member needs to:

★ Fight in hand-to-hand combat
★ Speak a second language
★ Have excellent navigation skills
★ Have a thorough knowledge of weapons and their use
★ Be an expert in their specialism such as flying or electronics.

Training in water

Women in the Special Forces

In recent years, women have been allowed to join the Special Forces in countries such as Australia, France and the United States. Reportedly, China has a women-only Special Forces unit. British law preventing women from joining the Special Forces will be reviewed in 2018.

Trainee operatives must be expert at wading through rivers carrying heavy kit.

Special Forces teams are not just looking for men and women who show bravery in dangerous situations. They are also looking for people who have the extraordinary mental strength needed to make life-or-death decisions.

During training, the recruits find out what it is like to be isolated from their team, to be responsible for the safety of others in the unit and to undertake exhausting physical challenges having had only a few hours sleep. Recruits endure days of training in realistic scenarios of assaults, shootouts and hostage situations.

Checking location

operatives lose focus, or panic in training they will not make it. Have a member of the elite fails to use body armour or gun in a real situation would risk their own death, that of team members and the failure of the mission. For those few who do qualify the training never stops. Every commando has to keep in top mental and physical form and will undergo training wherever they are not in action. SAS operatives who are newly qualified have to serve a probation period as they continue training. Even at this stage, there are still soldiers who are returned to unit

THINK LIKE A SPECIAL FORCES OPERATIVE

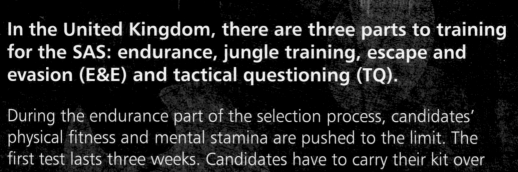

In the United Kingdom, there are three parts to training for the SAS: endurance, jungle training, escape and evasion (E&E) and tactical questioning (TQ).

During the endurance part of the selection process, candidates' physical fitness and mental stamina are pushed to the limit. The first test lasts three weeks. Candidates have to carry their kit over long, timed hikes, navigating between checkpoints. The next section in the endurance phase is a 64-kilometre trek carrying a 25-kilogram rucksack. This trek must be completed in fewer than 24 hours.

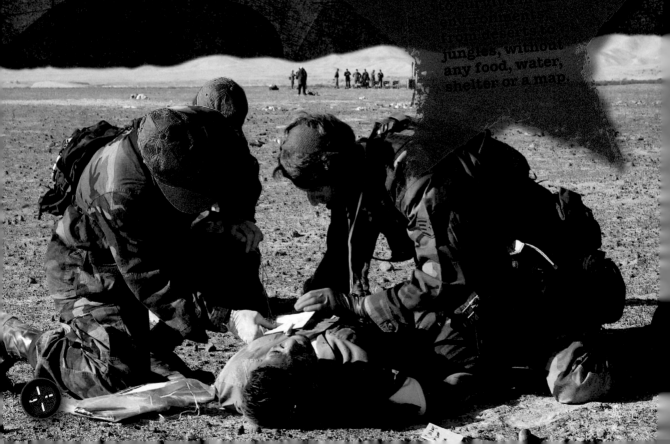

Recruits train to survive in all environments, from deserts to jungles, without any food, water, shelter or a map.

Harder and harder

The candidates who pass the first phase of training then move on to jungle training. This takes place in the heart of the Belize jungle. Trainees have to live for weeks behind enemy lines, surviving on rations. This stage of the training tests candidates' physical and mental abilities.

The few candidates who have passed the first two stages progress to the final phase of the process. In the E&E section of the course, candidates have to find their way to a series of waypoints without being captured by other soldiers. After three days, whether they have been captured or not, candidates report for TQ. This tests operatives' ability to cope during interrogation by enemies.

Working as a team

ACT LIKE A SPECIAL FORCES OPERATIVE

TAKE THE TEST!

Would you pass training?

You now know what it takes to get through the Special Forces training. Do you think you have what it takes? Check your memory, which is important for special ops work, by taking this test:

Q1. What is the first part of the SAS training called?

Q2. How long do candidates have to complete the trek in phase one of SAS training?

Q3. Name four countries that allow women to join the Special Forces.

Q4. Special Forces trainees need to prove they have physical strength. What other strength do they need to demonstrate?

Q5. What does E&E stand for?

Q6. What must you be a member of before applying for a role with the Special Forces?

Q7. Name two key skills a Special Forces operative needs to have.

Q8. What happens if you do not pass one stage of the training?

ANSWERS

CHAPTER 4: Teamwork

There is no place in the Special Forces for anyone who does not work well in a team. Each person has individual expertise needed by the team and the team is trained to work together.

As well as those active in missions, there is a huge organisation behind the frontline team. Members analyse intelligence, help to prepare for the mission and if necessary, watch and wait until the go-ahead for a mission is given. Others make sure each team has the best and most up-to-date weapons, equipment and support.

Operatives on the frontline

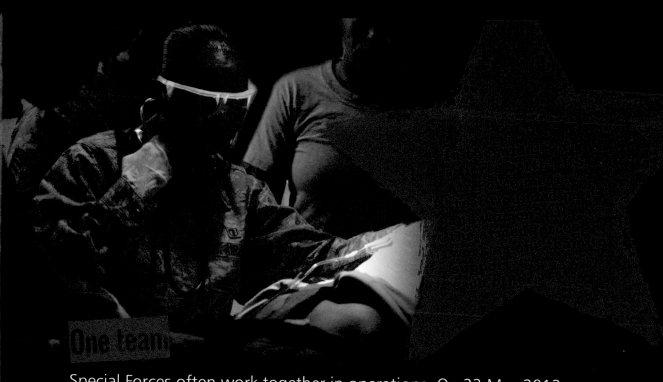

One team

Special Forces often work together in operations. On 22 May 2012, British aid worker Helen Johnston and three of her colleagues were captured in a remote part of Afghanistan. The kidnapped women were held hostage in caves. Using a drone, SAS commanders and intelligence officers surveyed the area where the women were being held. A force of 28 members of the SAS and 28 US Navy Seals was formed to rescue Miss Johnston and her colleagues. The team rehearsed and planned for every eventuality before being given the go-ahead for the rescue operation. On 31 May, the operation was successfully completed – the four women were rescued alive and the kidnappers were killed.

THINK LIKE A PILOT

Deployment

Today's Special Forces operatives are kitted out with the best and most up-to-date equipment, from night vision goggles to lightweight lethal weaponry. In some situations, Special Forces operatives have no backup equipment. Then, they must rely on their survival skills.

Special Forces operatives need to penetrate enemy territory without detection. To do this, they drop from aircraft at heights of around 8,000 metres. Specially designed parachutes allow them to glide great distances before dropping onto their landing point. This is called High Altitude High Opening (HAHO). In other types of jumps agents free-fall for long distances before opening their parachutes at the last minute. This is called High Altitude Low Opening (HALO). Jumpers take in oxygen from special helmets. Without this, they could die in the thin atmosphere at this altitude.

Special forces teams carry radios to help them to keep in contact with their team and HQ. On a mission, they may enter what looks like a deserted village and often have to radio to alert if they discover dangers. Their radios can be attached to their waistcoat or helmet.

Special Forces, including the SEALs and SAS, train their own tracker dogs. These dogs are excellent at finding buried explosive devices or hidden enemies. The animals are strapped to their trainers as they parachute into hostile territory.

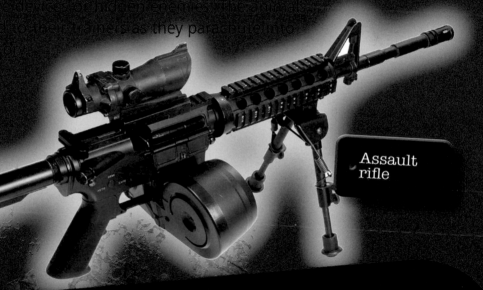

Assault
rifle

THINK LIKE AN SAS TEAM

TAKE THE TEST!

You need to pay attention to detail – test your powers of observation by answering these questions based on what you have read:

Q1. What does HAHO stand for?

Q2. What does HALO stand for?

Q3. Why is oxygen needed for some parachute jumps?

Q4. Why are dogs sometimes used in hostile territory?

Q5. What do Special Forces operatives use to communicate with each other?

Q6. What kind of assault rifle does the SAS carry?

Q7. What is fast rope?

Q8. What did operatives use to carry out video surveillance of the area where Helen Johnston was being held?

ANSWERS

CHAPTER 5:
Danger and Survival

The very nature of Special Forces' work means high risk and danger. These men and women are operating in the toughest conditions to defend and protect their countrymen and women. Tragically, sometimes things go wrong and there are deadly consequences.

Troops will have the best preparation. This includes dress rehearsals in specially built replicas of areas where crucial missions take place. For example, in the hunt for terrorist leader Osama bin Laden, SEALs repeated practice runs of the operation in a replica of the compound where Osama bin Laden (see page 35) was believed to be hiding, before the green light was given for the real mission. Before a mission can go ahead, the following must be studied:

- Enemy capability – knowing what the enemy is capable of.

- Weather conditions – this will determine if it is safe to fly and how good visibility is.

- Environmental conditions, such as the tide and currents, which can have a huge impact on combat swimming.

During the war in Afghanistan, Special Forces operatives worked alongside military forces. It is thought that, altogether, there were more than 2,300 US military and Special Forces deaths in Afghanistan.

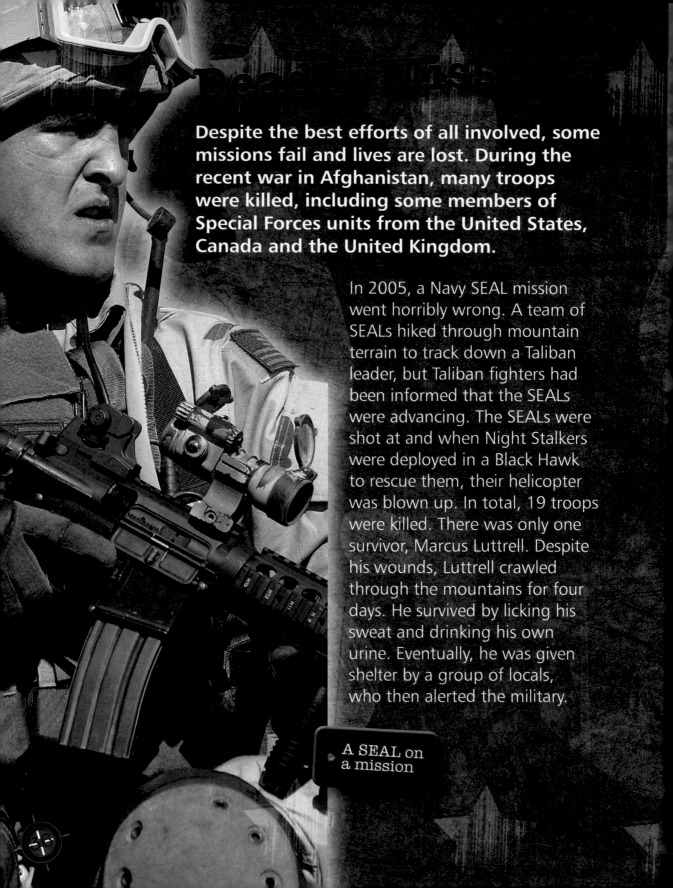

Deadly Missions

Despite the best efforts of all involved, some missions fail and lives are lost. During the recent war in Afghanistan, many troops were killed, including some members of Special Forces units from the United States, Canada and the United Kingdom.

In 2005, a Navy SEAL mission went horribly wrong. A team of SEALs hiked through mountain terrain to track down a Taliban leader, but Taliban fighters had been informed that the SEALs were advancing. The SEALs were shot at and when Night Stalkers were deployed in a Black Hawk to rescue them, their helicopter was blown up. In total, 19 troops were killed. There was only one survivor, Marcus Luttrell. Despite his wounds, Luttrell crawled through the mountains for four days. He survived by licking his sweat and drinking his own urine. Eventually, he was given shelter by a group of locals, who then alerted the military.

A SEAL on a mission

Tragedy

In December 2013, a Special Forces unit from the United Kingdom attacked a Taliban compound where terrorists were hiding. Most of the enemy were killed, but a lone gunman survived. He showered gunfire from an AK-47, which hit two Special Forces men and a military dog. The team leader, Captain Richard Holloway, was killed. One of the enemy targets killed during the mission was preparing for a suicide mission in the Afghan capital, Kabul.

Many Special Forces soldiers lost their lives in the Afghanistan conflict. So, too, did many Afghan civilians, innocently caught up in the war.

ACT LIKE A SURVIVOR

TAKE THE TEST!

Could you handle the pressure?

Can you remember what you have read about the risks and dangers that go hand in hand with work in the Special Forces?

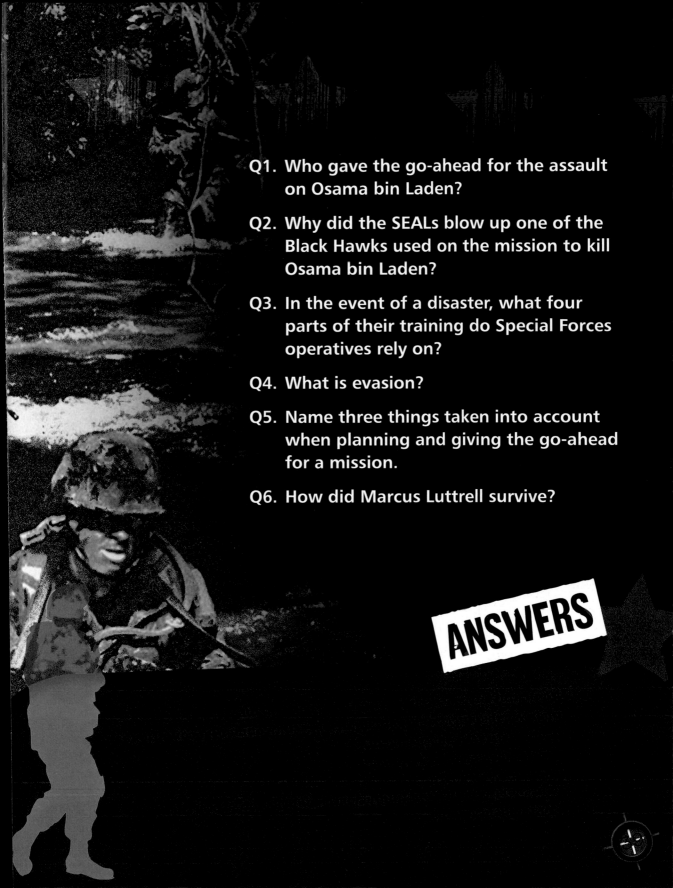

Q1. Who gave the go-ahead for the assault on Osama bin Laden?

Q2. Why did the SEALs blow up one of the Black Hawks used on the mission to kill Osama bin Laden?

Q3. In the event of a disaster, what four parts of their training do Special Forces operatives rely on?

Q4. What is evasion?

Q5. Name three things taken into account when planning and giving the go-ahead for a mission.

Q6. How did Marcus Luttrell survive?

ANSWERS

CHAPTER 6:
Global Elites

Elite forces have helped defend and protect nations for hundreds of years, across continents. Today, most countries have their own Special Forces to deal with the threat of terrorism or national crises. Members of these elite forces often work alongside their country's own army.

US Army medics treat a soldier.

D-Day

During the Second World War (1939–45) on 6 June 1944, an operation that had been years in the planning went ahead. Thousands of troops from the countries that were fighting Nazi Germany landed in German-occupied France. Among the troops were members from the US Army Rangers. The Rangers' job was to destroy German gun emplacements. In a carefully planned operation, British landing crafts dropped the Rangers at the bottom of the cliff. The Rangers scaled the cliffs of Pointe du Hoc, overlooking Omaha Beach. After destroying the guns, the Rangers bravely fought off the advancing Germans. After two days, only 90 of the 220 men were still alive.

Vietnam

During the long years of the Vietnam War (1954–75), Special Forces from the USA (including the Green Berets) and other countries, such as Australia and New Zealand, fought against the North Vietnamese in dense jungle. They also trained many South Vietnamese in combat skills. Eventually, the USA admitted defeat in the war, but the role of the Special Forces was largely acknowledged.

THINK LIKE A
SPECIAL FORCES OPERATIVE

Germany's Special Forces, called the GSG9, were formed in 1973 after a terrible attack a year earlier, when the country hosted the Olympic Games. During this attack, 11 Israeli athletes were kidnapped and killed. Today's GSG9 is reportedly so effective that in more than 1,500 missions, they have fired their weapons just five times.

SSG

Pakistan's SSG are known as 'Black Storks' because of their distinctive headgear. They are trained in hostage rescue, direct action, counter-terrorism and unconventional warfare.

Russian Spetsnaz

The Russian Special Forces ops are trained to endure physical pain. Many of the bodyguards for top Russian politicians are chosen from the Spetsnaz.

Pakistan's SSG commandos prepare for action.

SASR

Australia's Special Air Service Regiment (SASR) was formed in 1957. The number of members in the SASR is classified but it is reported to be around 600 personnel.

For good or bad?

Secrecy lies at the heart of the Special Forces. However, it is difficult to achieve a balance between the need for secrecy required to carry out effective missions and the need for openness for others to ensure that missions are carried out for the right reasons and with responsibility.

ACT LIKE A GIGN OPERATIVE

Have You Got What it Takes?

If you want to become a member of the Special Forces, following these steps is a good place to start.

School

Study hard to get your qualifications. Being a member of the Special Forces takes intelligence and hard work, not just physical strength. Study a second language, too.

Volunteer

Join clubs and groups that offer you the chance to improve your fitness and develop your team skills.

Qualifying

It takes a long time to qualify as a member of the Special Forces. You may decide the job is not for you, and that your skills are best used in other areas of the military.

Personality

Make sure your behaviour and actions are always responsible. There is no place in the Special Forces for people who break the law.

Fitness

Keep yourself in good physical shape.

Military

Special Forces operatives are all in the military. Think about which branch of the military you want to join, and apply.

AK-47 a semi-automatic and automatic assault rifle

analyse to study in detail

Army Rangers an elite airborne United States military arm

combat a fight, especially during a war

commandos soldiers in an elite force trained to carry out raids

compound a large area that includes houses

counter-terrorism work to combat the threat of terrorism

demolitions destroying or pulling down structures, often using explosive devices

elite special and exclusive

ground force troops on land

fast rope the technique of descending from a helicopter by climbing down a thick rope

hijacked taken control of

hostages people captured and held by others

insert to get Special Forces operatives into a target area

intel (short for intelligence), information about an enemy, its plans and its power

kit body armour and equipment

military to do with the armed forces

motto a phrase that sums up the key belief of an organisation or team

operative a person working in a Special Forces field

ops short for operation

rations limited amount of food

recruits people who have recently joined the military

sniper a skilled person with a gun, on the lookout and ready to shoot

Taliban an extremist Islamic group

terrain land

terrorist a person who uses violence to force a government to change

trademark a symbol that represents a team

unconventional warfare using tactics and methods that are not used in traditional or conventional warfare to defeat the enemy

For More Information

Books

Special Forces (100 Facts), John Farndon, Miles Kelly Publishing

Special Forces (Heroic Jobs), Ellen Labrecque, Raintree

Special Forces (Radar), Adam Sutherland, Wayland

Special Forces (Usborne Beginners Plus), Henry Brook, Usborne

Websites

This website for the United Kingdom's Special Forces has information and photos of operatives in action:
www.eliteukforces.info

Information on the Australian Special Forces can be found on this website:
www.army.gov.au/Our-people/Units/Special-Operations-Command

Visit this site to see the Green Berets in action:
http://channel.nationalgeographic.com/remembering-911/episodes/ inside-the-green-berets1

Note to parents and teachers
Every effort has been made by the Publisher to ensure that these websites contain no inappropriate or offensive material. However, because of the nature of the Internet, it is impossible to guarantee that the contents of these sites will not be altered. We strongly advise that Internet access is supervised by a responsible adult.

Index